Bind Us Together

Presented to:

....

From:

....

Date:

....

Bind Us Together

An Illustrated Treasury for Couples

Moody Press
Chicago

Typeset by Eagle
Printed in Singapore
ISBN No: 0 8024 2627 2

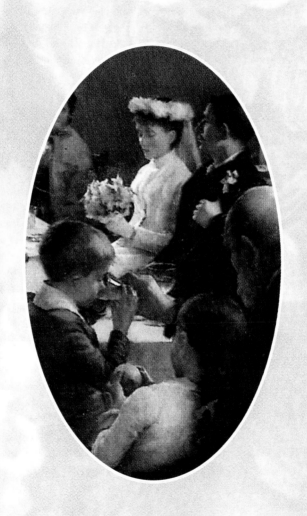

Contents

Love is very patient and kind, never jealous or envious, never boastful or proud, never haughty or selfish or rude. Love does not demand its own way. It is not irritable or touchy. It does not hold grudges and will hardly even notice when others do it wrong. It is never glad about injustice, but rejoices whenever truth wins out. If you love someone you will be loyal to him no matter what the cost. You will always believe in him, always expect the best of him, and always stand your ground in defending him.

1 Corinthians 13: 4-7 (LB)

Marriage

There is no more lovely, friendly
and charming relationship,
communion or company
than a good marriage.
Martin Luther

Marriage is given,
 that husband and wife may comfort
 and help each other,
 living faithfully together
in need and in plenty,
 in sorrow and in joy.
 It is given,
that with delight and tenderness
they may know each other in love,
and through the joy of their bodily union,
 may strengthen the union
of their hearts and lives.

       The Marriage Service

 Wives are young men's mistresses,
companions for middle age, and old men's
nurses.

       Francis Bacon

When two married people donate quality time to one another, they convey several non-verbal messages: you matter to me; our relationship matters to me, and I want our love to deepen with the years, not to fade or die.

And when a couple donate quality time to one another, both partners receive certain assurances: I am of sufficient worth to my partner for him or her to want to spend time with me; I am loved, and I am lovable. These are the most healing messages anyone in the world can hope to receive.

Joyce Huggett

We don't naturally grow together and love each other more. We tend to grow apart, to grow distant. So we have to work hard at marriage. It's the most fun work in the world, but still it's work.

Anne Ortlund

Newly Married

O Lord, we two want to begin our life together with you, and we want always to continue it with you.

Help us never to hurt and never to grieve one another.

Help us to share all our work, all our hopes, all our dreams, all our successes and all our failures, all our sorrows and all our joys. Help us to have no secrets from one another, so that we may be truly one.

Keep us always true to one another, and grant that all the years ahead may draw us ever closer to one another. Grant that nothing may ever come between us, and nothing may ever make us drift apart.

And, as we live with one another, help us to live with you, so that our love may grow perfect in your love, for you are the God whose name is love.

This we ask for your love's sake. Amen.

William Barclay

Men derive their sense of value from being trusted and admired, women derive theirs from being cared for.

David Riddell

Marriage is not merely a cultural invention, but God's perfect design for companionship.

R. Paul and Gail Stevens

Marriage is the alliance of two people, one of whom never remembers birthdays and the other never forgets them.

Ogden Nash

A Marriage Feast

Fast from criticism and feast on praise,
Fast from self-pity and feast on joy,
Fast from ill-temper and feast on peace,
Fast from resentment and feast on
    contentment
Fast from pride and feast on humility,
Fast from selfishness and feast on service,
Fast from fear and feast on faith.

Marion Stroud

When I have learnt to love God better than my earthly dearest, I shall love my earthly dearest better than I do now.

C.S. Lewis

Recipe for disaster: Hollywood idealism plus large doses of 'meism'. Unrealistic expectations of what a marriage should be like is marriage enemy number one. Selfishness follows as a close second.

David Riddell

Romance and tenderness die through neglect. Remember to nurture each other with little acts of kindness. Compete with each other to make each other happy.

David Riddell

L ord, we lay our differences before You. You created each of us unique for a special purpose. And yet You say that we also are to become one! Lord, that kind of harmony in our marriage would be a miracle that could come only from You. Make it happen, we pray, by Your Spirit. We place our lives into Your hands.

Roger and Donna Vann

He who finds a wife finds what is good and receives favor from the LORD.

Proverbs 18:22

Space is as essential to relationships as the gap between the rungs of the ladder.

Joyce Huggett

Happiness grows at our own firesides, and is not to be picked in strange gardens.

Douglas Jerrold

Be to her virtues very kind.
Be to her faults a little blind.

Matthew Prior

An archaeologist is the best husband any woman can have. The older she gets, the more interested he is in her.

Agatha Christie

That is how husbands should treat their wives, loving them as part of themselves. No one hates his own body but lovingly cares for it . . . So . . . a man must love his wife as part of himself.

Ephesians 5:25–33

A woman was not made out of his head to top him, nor out of his feet to be trampled upon by him; but out of his side, to be equal to him; under his arm to be protected; and near his heart to be loved.

Matthew Henry

If you are a husband and father, come alongside your wife to protect her and support her. Crossing the turbulent waters of child rearing together will strengthen your mate's self-esteem and bring you to the empty nest united.

Dennis Rainey

Can two walk together, except they be agreed?

Amos 3:3

Some people are more courteous to complete strangers than they are to their life-time companions.

David Riddell

A threefold cord is not easily broken – invite Jesus Christ to become that third strand. He is the creator and sustainer of the institute of marriage, and His kind of love must be learnt.

David Riddell

Marriage and how to manage it: Communicate, decide things together, be kind and tender, have time for yourself, and together. Be romantic – even foolish, have similar interests, be sensible with money but occasionally be rash. Surprise each other and have humor, and fun, but mostly – ENJOY!

Simon Bond

Wives who want to dominate their husbands should remember: a man may not be a husband to his 'mother'.

David Riddell

And if your hearts are bound together by love; if both are yielding and true; if both cultivate the spirit of meekness, forbearance, and kindness, you will be blessed in your home and in the journey of life.

Matthew Hale

True romance, the special attraction between a husband and wife, was God's original idea. He invented it to be free of lust, exploitation, or disappointment. In the Song of Solomon, the writer speaks of the beautiful, powerful attraction a wife has for her husband, 'Let him kiss me with kisses of his mouth — for your love is more delightful than wine.'

Robert and Cheryl Moeller

Money

*But seek first his kingdom and his
righteousness, and all these things will
be given to you as well. Therefore do not
worry about tomorrow, for tomorrow
will worry about itself. Each day has
enough trouble of its own.*
Matthew 6:33, 34

Lord, we covenant together now in Your
presence to seek You first, to put You
ahead of any material gain. We accept the
fact that we are simply temporary man-
agers of the money and possessions You
have given us. We want to give generously
to others under Your leadership. We trust
You to meet our daily needs and to lead us
into financial freedom.

Roger and Donna Vann

I have never counseled a dying man who
regretted not having made more money,
but quite a few regretted not having spent
enough time with their families.

Charles Swindoll

Oh God, give us more faith in your abundance.

Help us to stop worrying about money so much. Let us spend less time fretting about material things.

We often envy other people their possessions. Forgive us. We do not covet – no, for we don't wish them less. Only we are anxious for more, so much more. And this is wrong.

It is putting emphasis on the wrong things. It shows our lack of faith.

Lord, help us to remember how generously you have endowed the earth. That you have lavished upon us more food than any of us can consume. More clothing than any of us can wear. More treasures than we can carry.

Marjorie Holmes

On an Anniversary

O God, I can hardly believe that the time has gone so quickly. And here I am remembering once more, the day when first this special happiness came to me. It doesn't seem long—save that so much has happened.

I thank you for every supporting experience of love and consideration. I thank you for happy surprises that have broken in upon this year, for every tie strengthened, every joy doubled because freely shared.

There are things I wish I hadn't to remember, some words I wish I hadn't spoken, some thoughts I wish I hadn't turned over in my mind, some things I wish I hadn't done.

Forgive me, I pray, and let me put behind me anything which has marred this year together; and give me good sense and loving strength not to do any of these things again. Amen

Rita Snowden

A wife can often surprise her husband on their wedding anniversary by mere-ly mentioning it.

E.C. McKenzie

O God, we thank you that you have given us another year of life together.
We thank you
For the love which grows more precious
    and for the bonds
which grow more close each day.
We thank you
For the happiness we have known together;
For the sorrows we have faced together;
For all the experiences of sunshine and of
    shadow through which we have come
    today.
We ask for your forgiveness
For any disloyalty;
For any times when we were difficult to
    live with;
For any selfishness and inconsiderateness;
For any lack of sympathy and of
    understanding;
For anything which spoiled even for a
    moment the perfect relationship
    which marriage should be.
Spare us to each other to go on walking
the way of life together, and grant that for
us it may be true that the best is yet to be:
through Jesus Christ our Lord. Amen.

William Barclay (adapted)

Love

There are four things that are too
mysterious for me to understand:
an eagle flying in the sky,
a snake moving on a rock,
a ship finding its way over the sea,
and a man and a woman falling in love.
Proverbs 30:18 (GNB)

It is not surprising that the biblical descriptions of love are not what the world advertises. This love takes all that one has to practice it. This love doesn't come easily; it is not natural. As you begin to practice true love, you will see a transformation in yourself as well as in your loved one.

William L. Thrasher

To keep your marriage brimming
With love in the marriage cup,
Whenever you're wrong, admit it;
Whenever you're right, shut up.

Ogden Nash

A man is only told to study two things—his Bible and his wife—because both require interpretation. A woman puts out a lot of signals, especially as she goes through certain stages of life. If you don't read those signals right, Lord have mercy.

Tony Evans

Knowing how to love is important to good relationships. A man who is committed to a growing relationship knows how to express his love to his sweetheart: It means flowers, little surprises, sweet notes, a wink across a crowded room, a mid-morning phone call, a listening ear, and a word of encouragement.

Joseph Stowell

Hugging your spouse before she goes shopping may not only express love, it may bring her home sooner.

Gary Chapman

Sex creates a 'soul tie' beween two people, forming the most intimate of all human relationships. God intended that the first sexual experience be enjoyed by a man and a woman who are wholly committed to each other with the protection of a covenant. That was to assure the acceptance and unconditional love that guard the most intimate of all human relationships.

Erwin Lutzer

Humor is a vital element in preventing marital failure. The ability to laugh does not mean being a class clown or even a joke teller. In fact, the poor guy may be hopeless at telling jokes, needing the woman's help when he forgets punch lines and gets vacant stares. But it *is* important that he likes to laugh.

Alistair Begg

Forgiveness

When I have been wronged by my
spouse and she has painfully confessed
it and requested forgiveness, I have
the option of justice or forgiveness.
Forgiveness is the way of love.
Gary Chapman

Be humble and gentle. Be patient with each
other, making allowance for each other's
faults because of your love . . . Don't let the
sun go down with you still angry — get over it
quickly . . . Quarreling, harsh words, and dis-
like of others should have no place in your
lives. Instead, be kind to each other, tender-
hearted, forgiving one another, just as God
has forgiven you . . .

Ephesians 4: 2, 26, 31–32 (LB)

If we knew that life would end tomorrow
. . . but who can say that it will not? The only
time of which we can be certain is today. So
today I will reach out for your hand. Today I
will say 'I'm sorry' and 'I love you.'

Marion Stroud

There is no hope for happiness in harboring hurt feelings or thoughts. In marriage of all places we cannot live in the past. We must, if we are to be happy together, learn the discipline of forgiving and forgetting. In marriage we cannot allow ourselves to be chained to yesterday's mistake or last year's failure.

John Drescher

Communication

Choose your tone of voice more carefully,
for it communicates more than
your choice of words.
David Riddell

The six most important words—
I am sorry, I was wrong
The five most important words—
You did it very well
The four most important words—
What do you think?
The three most important words—
I love you
The two most important words—
Thank you
The one most important word—
We
The least important word—
I

Marion Stroud

Thank you, God, for teaching us to talk to one another. Thank you for the gift of words. Thank you for each other with whom to share our hopes, our fears, our problems and our plans. Banish our fear of ridicule or rejection, so that we can be totally honest, completely ourselves.

Thank you for showing us the need to listen. To listen with our hearts as well as with our ears, sensing the needs that may remain unspoken. To know that when there are no words to meet the situation, then love can be a silent song — a touch that says 'I'm in this situation with you,' a smile that reassures, 'You're doing fine.'

Thank you that we have learned the need for patience. Thank you for teaching a talkative partner brevity, and a quieter one how to express himself.

We often struggle with this vital task of real communication. But thank you God for teaching us to talk to one another. Thank you for the gift of words.

Marion Stroud

*Think of all the squabbles
Adam and Eve must have had in
the course of their nine hundred
years. Eve would say, 'You ate
the apple,' and Adam would
retort, 'You gave it to me.'*

Martin Luther

Dear Lord, again we are reminded of our human tendency to attack and accuse, when we need to accept and forgive. Let our heart's desire be to minister to each other, rather than to manipulate. Thank You for forgiving us completely, because of what Jesus did on the cross. Guide us in the coming months, so that we may see the barriers between us coming down.

Roger and Donna Vann

Dear Lord, thank you for the good days of marriage. The days when we wake up pleased with each other, our jobs, our children, our homes and ourselves.

Thank you for our communication—the times when we can really talk to each other, and the times when we understand each other without so much as a gesture or a word.

Thank you for our companionship—the time when we can work together at projects we both enjoy. Or work in our separate fields and yet have that sense of sharing that can only come when two people's lives have merged in so many other ways, so long.

Thank you for our times of privacy. Our times of freedom. Our relaxed sense of personal trust.

Thank you that we don't have to clutch and stifle each other, that we have learned to respect ourselves enough to respect the other's individuality.

Thank you, Lord, that despite the many storms of marriage we have reached these particular shores.

Marjorie Holmes

A life of prayer with your spouse can allow you to plumb the depths of your relationship far beyond what most people ever experience. You can enter into a world of spiritual reality and power that very few venture into or explore.

Robert and Cheryl Moeller

Discover and cultivate an interest that both of you can enjoy.

David Riddell

And if your hearts are bound together by love; if both are yielding and true; if both cultivate the spirit of meekness, forbearance, and kindness, you will be blessed in your home and in the journey of life.

Matthew Hale

Parenthood

*The most important thing a father
can do for his children is to
love their mother.*
Theodore M. Hesburgh

Father, we know that children are a gift
from You. Is this a gift that you are
going to give us? Would You please pre-
pare us for such a responsibility. Any children we might have need us to be a solid
unit, secure in each other and in You. We
commit to You the timing of this amazing
miracle of new life. May we learn from You
all we need to know in order to love, nurture and teach our children.

Susan Wavre

Children truly are God's most precious
gift to His people, even with the trials and
tribulations they bring with them. Parents
have only one chance to raise their children.
If they squander it, they will regret it the
rest of their lives.

Larry Burkett

Father, we as parents need to live each day, each minute, yielded to You. Teach us to walk moment by moment in the power of Your Spirit, that our lives and our family might bring honor to You. Remind us to pray daily for our children.

Roger and Donna Vann

A torn jacket is soon mended; but hard words bruise the heart of a child.

Longfellow

Please show us God how to give our child those precious but invisible gifts — roots and wings; security and freedom.

We know that he will need to feel secure; to sense that we will always love him come what may. But we're just human beings — beginners in the school of parenthood. There are may be times when we don't feel so loving, when daily life is just too 'daily"and the fabric of our family life gets frayed around the edges. Help us to know that if human parents get it wrong from time to time, we can all depend completely on our Heavenly Father.

Marion Stroud

Tender touch, supporting words, quality time, gifts, and acts of service all converge to meet your child's need of love. If that need is met and your child genuinely feels loved, it will be far easier to learn and respond in other areas.

Gary Chapman and Ross Campbell

Home and Family

As for me and my house,
we will serve the LORD.
Joshua 24:15 (KJ)

God bless this house from roof to floor
God bless the windows and the door
God bless us all for evermore
God bless the house with fire and light
God bless each room with thy might
God with thy hand keep us right
God be with us in this dwelling site.

David Adam

Heavenly Father, we thank you for our neighbors and for the people around us with whom we share our daily lives.

We pray for those who are old and lonely; those isolated because of ill-health; and those who find it difficult to make friends.

Show us what we can do to help, and teach us to be good neighbors; for Jesus' sake.

Llewellyn Cumings

Forgive us, O Lord
For everything that has spoiled our home
life:
For the moodiness and irritability which
made us difficult to live with;
For the insensitiveness which made us care-
less of the feelings of others;
For selfishness which made life harder for
others.

Forgive us, O Lord,
For everything that has spoiled our witness
for You;
That so often men would never have known
that we had been with Jesus and pledged
ourselves to Him:
That we have so often denied with our lives
that which we said with our lips;
For the difference between our creed and our
conduct, our profession and our practice;
For any example which made it easier for men
to criticise Your church or for another to
sin.

We thank you for Jesus Christ our Savior. Strengthen us by your Spirit that in the days to come, we may live more as we should. Through Jesus Christ our Lord. Amen.

William Barclay (adapted)

Family Harmony

How sweet it is, Lord, when people live in harmony.

Bless our family members so that they may make beautiful music together at home.

Let our communication be open, loving.

Strengthen our marriage bond.

Help our children to honor us their parents, Lord,

and confide in us.

May discord and strife never overcome us.

Let our conversations be occasions of joy.

May kind words refresh our minds and hearts.

Let each of us make a positive contribution by generosity and unselfishness.

You are the unseen member of all families.

Joseph T. Sullivan (adapted)

Happy Families

There is no such thing as a 'perfect family', and happiness does not come gift-wrapped. But a truly happy family can be created when each member of that family resolves to put these principles into practice:

1. We will not try to take the little things of daily life for granted, but will show our appreciation, both by our words and actions, of clothes that are washed, meals that are cooked, and financial needs that are supplied.

2. We will accept that just as the pleasures and comforts of home life are equally available to all, so are the chores and responsibilities, and we will each do our share without grumbling.

3. We will look for something to praise before we criticise, and when criticism is necessary, we will make sure that it is constructive. We will aim to build up rather than to tear down.

4. We will recognise the importance of effort as well as of achievement and praise both equally.

5. We will not offer more kindness, consideration and understanding to those outside the family that to those within it.

'Please', 'Thank you' and 'I love you' will often be said amongst us.

6. We will not demand perfection in the behavior of other family members until we can offer it to them ourselves. When we are bad-tempered or in the wrong we will admit it and apologise.

7. We will try to remember at all times that people matter more than things. This being so, we will not covet our neighbor's stereo, new car, foreign holidays, kitchen gadgets, electronic marvels, income tax rebate, promotion or anything else that is theirs. Instead we will give it first place to the development of the qualities valued by God: love, joy, peace, patience, kindness, faithfulness, gentleness and self-control.

8. We will accept our home and the people in it as God's specially chosen gift to us, perfectly designed for our growth and development as individuals. We will encourage and believe in one another, accepting the need for risks, the possibility of failure, but also the potential for success if we set our prayerfully on this perilous but exciting enterprise of being a family.

Marion Stroud

CLAUDE STRACHAN

Home Harmony

There is no place like home.
We want it to be a special place, Lord,
  a sanctuary, a haven of peace.
Of course, it isn't always like that.
Behind the front door lies challenges,
  problems.
Harmony and forgiveness don't just happen;
  they must be cultivated.
Kindness is to be spoken within these walls.
There has to be give and take—
  expressions like 'I'm sorry,' and 'I love you.'
Be present in this home, Lord,
  and fill it with Your love.
May we be mindful of Your loving presence.

                              Joseph T. Sullivan

Every day in our fractured society
  we meet friends, relatives, and neighbors
  whose lives have been disrupted.
Help those whose dreams have been
  shattered
  to repair the psychological damage,
  and be reunited by Your grace.
Watch over them with loving care
  and bless them with renewed confidence.

                              Joseph T. Sullivan

In the Morning

Let your blessing today, O God, be with all
those who cross over our doorstep:
All who go out to attend to their affairs,
All who come in for any reason;
Those going out to the bustle of the world,
Those coming in to the warmth of the
family circle.

We rejoice in the intimated joys of our home;
In its safety and comfort and situation;
In its security of good relationships;
In its challenges shared and its strong
supporting love.
We rejoice that personal values are here
recognised
That the secret desires of any are the
concern of all;
That the successes of any are the pride of
all;
That the experiences of any are freely
shared with all.
We rejoice in the many outside interests
which center in our home:
In friends and acquaintances who find
here a good spirit;
In music and books and good talk;
In laughter and fun and family jokes.

Rita Snowden (adapted)

Dear Christ, bless our home. Come and be our guest, for where you are there must be peace. Help us to make our home a sanctuary where You are lovingly worshiped. Help us to be full of gentleness and affection in all our family relationships. Make Your influence be felt by all those who come under our roof, and let all beauty and tenderness be centered here. Amen.

Floyd Tompkins

Spirituality

Be still, and know that I am God.
Psalm 46:10

Lord, help us to make time for what is
important,
to set priorities and strive after them.
As we review our day, we know only too
well how crowded each day can become.
Being 'too busy' suffocates thoughtfulness
and sharing.
Families suffer, husbands and wives grow
apart,
and children are neglected.
Runaway ambition strangles loving
relationships,
and selfishness takes many forms.
Lord, our orientation is on the right track
when centered on You.
Help us to seek first Your kingdom;
then all other matters will fall into place.

Joseph T. Sullivan

Great is the LORD and most worthy of praise.
Psalm 145:3

Take time to praise God together. One way of doing this is to choose a psalm that is full of praise to God (such as Psalm 103 or 145—there are many more) and read it together, or use it as a guide for your own words.

The LORD is gracious and compassionate, slow to anger and rich in love.
Psalm 145:8

Father, we realise that our marriage must take second place to the relationship each of us has with You. Help us grow closer and closer to You; let Your Holy Spirit have His way in our lives, that Christ might be lifted up in and through us. We want to see in our marriage a oneness that only You can bring.

Roger and Donna Vann

Eternal God, we come, we come again,
seeking, hoping, wanting to hear Your
word.

We come because, despite our best efforts,
we have failed to live by bread alone.

We come impelled by a desire too deep for
    words,
with longings that are too infinite to express.

We come yearning for meaning in our existence
and purpose for our lives.

We come acknowledging our need for each
    other's
affirmation and encouragement, understanding
    and love.

We come confessing our dependence on You.
Lord, embrace us with Your forgiveness, and
    claim us
by the mystery and depths of Your love. Amen

Terry Falla

Do not give to a man or woman what belongs to God – your adoration, your security, your entire sense of worth as a person.

David Riddell

In the name of Jesus Christ, who was never in a hurry, we pray, O God, that You would slow us down, for we know that we live too fast. With all of eternity before us, make us take time to live—time to get acquainted with You, time to enjoy Your blessings, and time to know each other.

Peter Marshall (adapted)

Lord, we admit that we have sometimes been more interested in getting our own way than in letting You have Your way with us. Draw us closer to Yourself. Fill us anew with your Spirit, that we might have the strength to yield to one another out of the overflow of our relationship with you.

Roger and Donna Vann

Dear Lord and Father of mankind,
Forgive our foolish ways.
Re-clothe us in our rightful mind,
In purer lives thy service find,
    In deeper reverence, praise.

In simple trust like theirs who heard,
    Beside the Syrian sea,
The gracious calling of the Lord,
Let us, like them, without a word,
    Rise up and follow Thee.

Drop thy still dews of quietness,
    Till all our strivings cease;
Take from our souls the strain and stress,
And let our ordered lives confess
    The beauty of Thy peace.
                    John Greenleaf Whittier

Lord Jesus our Savior,
let us now come to You;
our hearts are cold;
    Lord, warm them by Your selfless love;
our hearts are sinful;
    cleanse them with Your precious blood.
Our hearts are weak;
    strengthen them with Your joyous
    Spirit.
Our hearts are empty;
    fill them with Your divine presence.
Lord Jesus, our hearts are Yours;
    possess them always
    and only for
    Yourself.

                                    St Augustine of Hippo

Teach us, good Lord, to serve You as You
deserve; to give and not to count the
cost; to fight and not to heed the wounds; to
toil and not to seek for rest; to labor and not
to ask for any reward, save that of knowing
that we do Your will; through Jesus Christ
our Lord.

                                    Ignatius of Loyola

Morning

O God, it seems no time since we put out
the light and now the new day has
come;
We rejoice in the renewal of sleep;
We rejoice in another chance to think and
feel;
We rejoice in another chance to love and
serve.

While we enjoy our home and family, let us
not be unmindful of many needy ones
in Your world family:
All who lack knowledge of Your Gospel:
All who lack clothing and food and
shelter;
All who lack work to do and a hope to
fasten on.

We pray especially for all who face this day
without health and strength of body or
mind:
All who start it without interest;
All who face the earning of money with
anxiety;
All hindered, and hurt by alcoholism,
and any other secret addiction.

Guide and encourage in your on good
      way,
      all who approach new responsibilities
      this day, shy, or unsure:
      All who receive little new lives into
      their care;
      All who are taking examinations,
      having done their best;
      All setting out on long journeys,
      nervous of their reception,

Whatever our special needs, Your wisdom
      and love and care are sufficient.
Whatever we are called to go through,
      nothing can utterly overwhelm us.
In this security of spirit, is our strength,
      now and always.
      Amen

                  Rita Snowden

Evening

In this quietness we would take time to look
back over the day:
That Jesus has shown us what your very
      nature is,
      has made all the difference to this day;
That Jesus has taught us to call You 'Father',
      has made all the difference to this day;
That Jesus has declared himself our Savior
and Lord triumphant,
      has made all the difference to this day:
That we have been called to witness to these
      great securities,
      has made all the difference to this day.

Forgive us for anything foolish we've been
      responsible for today.
Forgive us for anything we have allowed to
      worry us
      as though we did not know You.
Forgive us for any required task we have
      shirked,
      any decision we have evaded.
Forgive us if we have taken refuge in a lame
      excuse or a lie.
Forgive us if we have expected from others
      far more than we have been ready to give.
Forgive us if we have gossiped, or wasted our
      time,
      forgetting the high hopes with which we

started the day.
In Your presence, we own our faults: ____ and
____ and we renew our vows.
Grant us your peace now. Amen

Rita Snowden (adapted)

God, make each moment of our lives a miracle; God, make us laugh at the utterly impossible; God, give us hope when all things seem hopeless, peace where no peace could be, love for the unlovable. Make us to gamble on all Your Almightiness, and to dare everything in Your great service.

M.E. Procter

O Lord my God, thank you
for bringing this day to a close;
Thank you for giving me rest
in body and soul.
Your hand has been over me
and has guarded and preserved me.
Forgive my lack of faith
and any wrong that I have done today,
and help me to forgive all who have
wronged me.
Let me sleep in peace under your protection,
and keep me from all the temptations of
darkness.
Into your hands I commend my loved
ones and all who dwell in this house; I
commend to you my body and soul. O
God, your holy name be praised. Amen.

Dietrich Bonhoeffer

Give us courage, O Lord, to stand up and be counted,

to stand up for those who cannot stand up for themselves,

to stand up for ourselves when it is needful for us to do so.

Let us fear nothing more than we fear You.

Let us love nothing more than we love You,

for thus we shall fear nothing also.

Let us have no other God before You, whether

nation or party or state or church.

Let us seek no other peace but the peace which is Yours,

and make us its instruments,

opening our eyes and our ears and our hearts, so that we should know always what work of peace we may do for You.

Alan Paton

Credits

Care has been taken to attribute all quotes from all sources, and to clear all permissions. We are grateful to the following for their permission and apologise for any unintentional omissions. The full works of the Moody Press authors quoted is also listed.

Adam, David: p 11, from a prayer card published by Tim Tiley Prints, Bristol; p 53, *The Edge of Glory* (London: Triangle, 1985).

Barclay, William: pp 12, 31, 54, *More Prayers for the Plain Man* (London: Fontana, 1969).

Begg, Alistair, p 37: works published by Moody Press: *What Angels Wish They Knew: The Basics of True Christianity*, 1999; *Lasting Love: How to Avoid Marital Failure*, 1997; *Made for His Pleasure: Ten Benchmarks of a Vital Faith*, 1996.

Bonhoeffer, Dietrich: p 81, *Letters and Papers from Prison* (London: SCM Press, 1971).

Burkett, Larry, p 48; works published by Moody Press: *Money Matters Software*, 1998; *Solar Flare (Christian Mystery)*, 1998; *Finding the Career That Fits You: The Companion Workbook to Your Career in Changing Times*, 1998; *Your Child Wonderfully Made: Discovering God's Unique Plan*, 1998; *Money Management for College Students*, 1998; *Money Matters for Teens Workbook: Age 11-14*, 1998; *Money Matters for Teens Workbook: Age 15-18*, 1998; *Giving and Tithing: Includes Serving and Stewardship*, 1998; *Personal Finances: Includes Family Budget Models*, 1998; *The Financial Guide for the Single Parent*, 1997; *Debt-Free Living: How to Get out of Debt (and Stay out)*, 1997; *The Financial Guide for the Single Parent workbook*, 1997; *Larry Burkett's Bill Organizer*, 1997; *Caretakers of God's Blessings: Using Our Resources Wisely (The Stewardship Series)*, 1996; *Where Your Treasure Is: Your Attitude on Finances (The Stewardship Series)*, 1996; *Hope When It Hurts: A Personal Testimony of How to Deal with the Impact of Cancer*, 1996; *Money before Marriage: A Financial Workbook for Engaged Couples*, 1996; *Women Leaving the Workplace: How to Make the Transition from Work to Home*, 1995; *Larry Burkett's Cash Organizer: Envelope Budgeting System*, 1995; *The Word on Finances: Topical Scriptures and Commentary*, 1994; *The Coming Economic Earthquake: Revised and Expanded for the Clinton Agenda*, 1994; *Your Career in Changing Times*, 1993; *Your Finances in Changing Times*, 1993; *The Family Budget Workbook: Gaining Control of Your Personal Finances*, 1993; *Victory over Debt: Rediscovering Financial Freedom*, 1992; *The Financial Planning Organizer: A Complete Budgeting Resource*, 1991; *Using Your Money Wisely: Biblical Principles under Scrutiny*, 1990; *The Financial Planning Workbook*, 1990; *How to Manage Your Money*, 1990; *Two Masters Video*, 1986; *How to Manage Your Money Workbook*, 1982.

Ross Campbell, p 51, *Parenting Your Adult Child: How You Can Help Them Achieve Their Full Potential*, (Chicago, Moody Press, 1999); *The Five Love Languages of Children*, (Chicago, Moody Press, 1998).

Chapman, Gary, p 38; works published by Moody Press: *The Other Side of Love: Handling Anger In A Godly Way*, 1999; *Parenting Your Adult Child: How You Can Help Them Achieve Their Full Potential*, 1999; *Loving Solutions: Overcoming Barriers in Your Marriage*, 1998; *Five Signs of a Loving Family*, 1998; *The Five Love Languages of Children*, 1997; *Toward a Growing Marriage: Building the Love Relationship of Your Dreams*, 1996; *Hope for the Separated: Wounded Marriages Can Be Healed*, 1996; *The Five Love Languages: How to Express Heartfelt Commitment to Your Mate*, 1992.

Drescher, John: p 39, from *The Gift of Marriage*, Marion Stroud (Oxford: Lion Publishing, 1982).

Evans, Tony, p 34: works published by Moody Press: *Who Is This King of Glory?: Experiencing The Fullness of Christ's Work in Our Lives*, 1999; *The Battle Is the Lord's: Waging Victorious Spiritual Warfare*, 1998; *What Matters Most: Four Absolute Necessities in Following Christ*, 1997; *Returning to Your First Love: Putting God Back in First Place*, 1995; *The Promise: Experiencing God's Greatest Gift*, 1996; *Our God is Awesome: Encountering the Greatness of Our God*, 1994; *Are Christians Destroying America?: How to Restore a Decaying Culture*, 1996; *Tony Evans Speaks Out On Divorce and Remarriage*, 1995; *Tony Evans Speaks Out On Gambling and the Lottery*, 1995; *Tony Evans Speaks Out On Sexual Purity*, 1995; *Tony Evans Speaks Out On Single Parenting*, 1995.

Falla, Terry: p 69, seen in *The Hodder Book of Christian Prayers*, Tony Castle (London: Hodder & Stoughton, 1986).

Holmes, Marjorie: pp 28, 44, *I've Got to Talk to Somebody, God* (London: Hodder & Stoughton, 1969)..

Huggett, Joyce: p 11, *Marriage Matters* (Guildford: Eagle Publishing, 1991); p 18, *Conflict* (Guildford: Eagle Publishing, 1998).

Lewis, C.S.: p 16, *Mere Christianity* (London: Fontana Books, 1952).

Lutzer, Erwin, p 37; works published by Moody Press: *Seven Reasons Why You Can Trust the Bible*, 1998; *Your Eternal Reward: Triumph and Tears at the Judgment Seat of Christ*, 1998; *Hitler's Cross: The Revealing Story of How the Cross of Christ Was Used As a Symbol of the Nazi Agenda*, 1998; *One Minute After You Die: A Preview of Your Final Destination*, 1997; *How You Can Be Sure that You Will Spend Eternity with God*, 1996; *Putting Your Past Behind You: Finding Hope for Life's Deepest Hurts*, Revised and Expanded edition 1997; *Christ Among Other Gods*, 1997; *The Serpent of Paradise: The Incredible Story of How Satan's Rebellion*

Serves God's Purposes, 1996; *No Place to Cry: The Hurt and Healing of Sexual Abuse*, 1990; *Dorie: The Girl Nobody Loved*, 1981.

Moeller, Robert and Cheryl, pp 24, 46, *Marriage Minutes: Inspirational Readings to Share with Your Spouse*, (Chicago, Moody Press, 1998).

Paton, Alan: p 82, seen in *The Hodder Book of Christian Prayers*, op. cit.

Procter, M.E.: p 81, seen in *The Hodder Book of Christian Prayers*, op. cit.

Rainey, Dennis, p 20; *Building Your Mate's Self-Esteem*, (Nashville, TH, Thomas Nelson Publishers, 1995).

Riddell, David, pp 15, 16, 18, 20, 23, 40, 46, 70, *Living Wisdom* (Guildford: Eagle Publishing, 1996).

Snowden, Rita: pp 29, 64, 75, 78, *Woman's Book of Prayers* (London: Fount, 1985).

Stowell, Joseph, p 34; works published by Moody Press: *Kingdom Conflict: Personal Triumph in a Supernatural Struggle*, Revised and Expanded edition 1996; *Far from Home: The Soul's Search for Intimacy with God*, 1998; *The Weight of Your Words: Measuring the Impact of What You Say*, 1998; *Perilous Pursuits: Our Obsession with Significance*, 1994; *Eternity: Reclaiming a Passion for What Endures*, 1997; *Loving Those We'd Rather Hate: Developing Compassion in an Angry World*, 1994; *Overcoming Evil with Good: The Impact of a Life Well-Lived*, 1995; *The Upside of Down: Finding Hope When It Hurts*, 1991; *Shepherding the Church: Effective Spiritual Leadership in a Changing Culture*, 1997.

Stroud, Marion: pp 16, 38, 41, 50, *The Gift of Marriage* (Oxford: Lion Publishing, 1994); p 40, *The Gift of Love* (Oxford: Lion Publishing, 1981); p 59, *The Gift of a Child* (Oxford: Lion Publishing, 1982).

Sullivan, Joseph T.: pp 56, 62, 66, *Good Night, Lord* (out of print). With kind permission of the author.

Swindoll, Charles: *The Grace Awakening* (Nashville, TN,Word Publishing, 1992).

Thrasher, William L.: p32, *Basics for Believers: Foundational Truths to Guide Your Life*, (Chicago, Moody Press, 1998).

Vann, Roger and Donna: pp 18, 27, 43, 50, 68, 70, *Secrets of a Growing Marriage* (San Bernardino, Ca: Here's Life Publishers, 1985).

Picture Credits

FAPL: Fine Art Picture Library Ltd

p 5, *The Health of the Bride (detail)*, Stanhope Forbes, 1857–1947, see p 17.

p 9, *A Wedding Morning*, 1892, John Henry F. Bacon, 1868–1914. Lady Lever Art Gallery, Port Sunlight.

p 13, *The Village Wedding*, 1883, Sir Luke Fildes, 1843–1927. The Manney Collection.

p 14, *Paris Street, A Rainy Day*, 1877 (detail), Gustave Caillebotte, 1848–1894. Art Institute of Chicago.

p 17, *The Health of the Bride*, 1889, Stanhope Forbes, 1857–1947. The Tate Gallery, London.

p 21, *The Europe Bridge*, 1876 (detail), Gustave Caillebotte, 1848–1894. Musée du Petit-Palais, Geneva.

p 22, *A Rally*, 1885, Sir John Lavery, RA, 1856–1941. Glasgow Art Gallery & Museum.

p 25, *In the Spring*, 1908–09, Harold Knight, 1974–1961. Tyne and Wear Museums, Newcastle upon Tyne.

p 26, *'Something Wrong Somewhere'*, 1868, Charles Green, RI, 1840–1898. Victoria & Albert Museum, London.

p 30, *In the Conservatory*, 1879, Eduoard Manet, 1832–1883. Nationalgalerie, Staatliche Museen, Berlin.

p 33, *Early Lovers*, 1858, Frederick Smallfield, 1829–1915. Manchester City Art Gallery.

p 35, *Halsway Court*, 1865 (detail), John William North, ARA, RWS, 1842–1924. Collection of Robin de Beaumont.

p 36, *The Village Wedding*, 1883 (detail), Sir Luke Fildes, see p 13.

p 39, *Recalling the Past*, 1888, Carlton Alfred Smith, RI, RWS, fl. 1871–1916. Victoria & Albert Museum, London.

pp 42, 43, *Resting in the Garden*, c.1914, Pierre Bonnard, 1867–1947. Nasjonagalleriet, Oslo.

p 45, *Where Next?*, Edward Frederick Brewtnall. Christopher Wood Gallery, London.

p 47, *'As cold water is to a thirsty soul, so is good news from a far country'*, 1864, George Smith, 1929–1901. Richard Green Gallery.

p 49, *Special Moments*, George Kilburne, 1839–1924. FAPL/Haynes Fine Art.

p 51, *The First Birthday Party*, 1867, Frederick Daniel Hardy, 1826–1911. Richard Green Gallery, London.

p 52, *At a Cottage Gate*, Helen Allingham, 1848–1926. Eagle Publishing.

p 55, *Watching the Porpoises*, 1863, Alfred Downing Fripp, RWS, 1822–1895. Bethnal Green Museum, London.